Happy Place

Joey Polisena

Published by Scorched Feathers
Willoughby, Ohio, USA

www.scorchedfeathers.com

Illustrations by Joey

Published by Scorched Feathers
Willoughby, OH
www.scorchedfeathers.com

PB ISBN: 979-8-9894772-2-7
HB ISBN: 979-8-9894772-5-8
eBook ISBN: 979-8-9894772-3-4
Audio ISBN: 979-8-9894772-4-1
Library of Congress Control Number: 2023921754

With you, floating on the breaths of these pages.

TABLE OF CONTENTS

FIRST KISS

She tastes like
marijuana and cabernet;
it's how she self-medicates
her lore, who she was before;
she rips this moment ablaze
and pulls me
sulfur-sparking all the way
further into her space;
her wild side is untied,
totally frayed
and I am magnetized,
can't pull myself away,
so I give in,
I stay,
I stay,
I stay,
let my brains fry
on her lips.

BEAUTIFULLY BROKEN

Unapologetically me—
I have to be:

survivor with frequent bleeds
from sharp edges
gorged to the bone
along stolen pieces,
the consequences
of other people's evils,
their unfulfilled needs
and unlearned lessons.

blindfolded and trying to read
the symbols and sketches—
I think it's Taiwanese
and trigonometry,
two of 7,096 languages
I don't speak.

It is what it is.
I try.
I grieve.

Thread my own needle
through my own skin,
grit to rip, again and again,
pull my wounds
into verses adrift
tinkling the stars
who catch a whiff,
stain their carpet

as I spark, and then
overfill our glasses,
seep through the cracks
with my glitter heart's
effervescence.

We may sparkle and fizz,
run headfirst into each other,
smother the next decade
in the lash, the fingertips
of our violet flames
until we burn out, flake
like paper-ball ash
in October wind;

or, maybe we don't start,
we don't put our toes at Go
because we know
we're just going to spin
and crash our ghosts,
explode, anyway.

It's hard
to love someone
who wasn't loved—
I know.

I try.
I grieve.

Here,
have a poem.

COME OVER

…and then we can fall asleep
wrapped up and reeking
of each other's dampened skin,
slide my toes along your shin,
release the ghosts of our needs,
our forgiven sinful energies,
and then,
fall into each other's dreams.

OPEN TO IT

You are not
a scream
into empty space,
there is something
that will catch your boom,
cradle your intensity
and send it back
with the same
tone and complexity,
because, baby,
nothing in this universe
is
without something
that needs it
to exist.

HALFWAY ALONE

Grown from stones
they muraled with shapes
that made us fit for display,
but we were so hollow
and so, I'm so undergrown
in spaces that seem to overflow
for others,
and then overgrown
in places where others don't know,
can't fathom
even when I ask them to imagine
being skipped across the surface
before going under.

I take no more chances
or rage in love with anyone
at dangerous paces.
All your intentions
will be sifted and weighed
and dusted and re-evaluated
for traces of love-bomb residue
imprinted into my skin
with burnt pins;

if I let your needle
stain my essence,
I need blood agreement
that you won't discard me
once I've let you in,
like they did:
gum in napkin.

I stay halfway alone,
will reliably
cut us off to the bone
at the first moment you derange,
slice away the tattoos
I suffered for you,
bleed and groan as the skin rips,
as I shape-shift
to trip you with my undertow,
splash you back into your place,
and crash you into my walls
of pretty stones;

and then I'll go on
all-the-way alone.

STUPID REPEAT

You are my insanity,
my stupid repeat
that drizzles in,
and then
thunders and sleets,
freezes to crush
just a few more pieces
every time you always
leave
a bigger space in me
that I insulate
and re-screen
and cement
and paint
and afix a twig
from a dead tree
like it's graffiti.

GHOST IN THE CARPET

We are red wine
kicked off an end table
in the fit of our deep,
oh, sweet,
"what-is-this?"
first kiss;
you and I will never
scrub what we are becoming
out of the rug fibers,
no, not when we've seeped
this way-too-far in
with lips and teeth
and legs
and fingertips,
unable to take a breath
let alone soak up the mess
quick enough
to ever be rid
of us.

WE SANG SONGS

When we sang songs,
everything was
We,
and now I think of you
when I sing.

LOVE ALWAYS

Daisy from our first date
pressed in a book that no one picks,
your photo shuffled into a frame
already fat with pictures,
crunchy crumbs I still nibble,
realize with my fingertips
every hand-slight chance I get,
…but I'll never admit it.

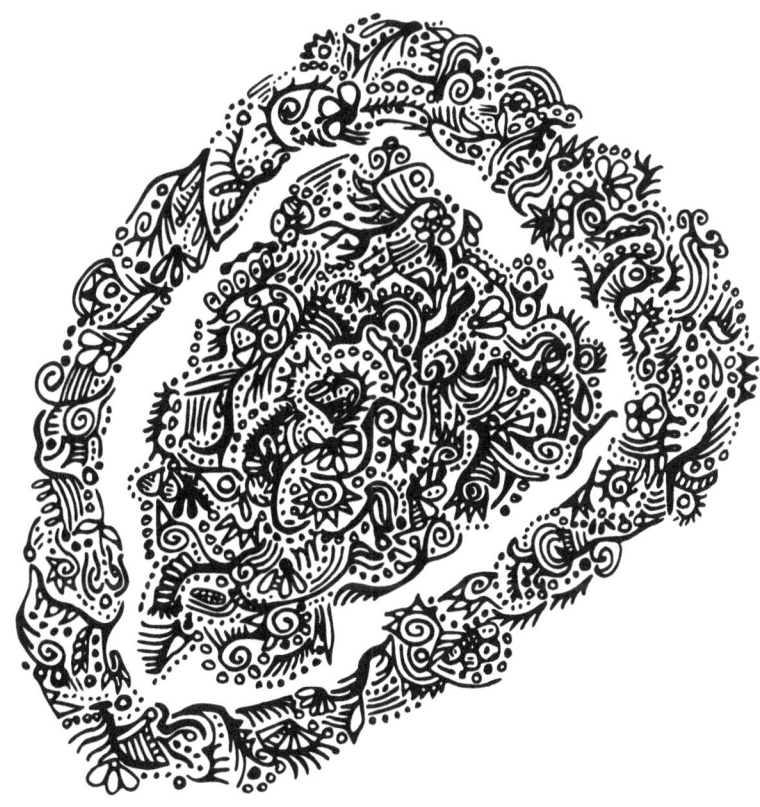

ALL MY MOURNING

I drenched another pillow
dreaming the words
we'll never speak to each other:
mystery symbolisms—
lost teeth,
that key behind a teacup
on a shelf in the kitchen—
logic blinds meanings,
none of it makes sense
and I try to weave
it into threads
to keep us connected,
bind you to stay
so we can say
everything;
I wake up with a scream
as I realize,
once again and forever,
all that talking to you
was just dreaming.

* * *

I drenched another pillow
remembering
every second
of begging for the love
you never had to give.

* * *

I drenched another pillow
in the nightmare fits
of all this sadness-
made-madness,
the remnants and ashes
of a world in chaos,
social posts
and smartphone streams
from both sides
of the sharpest divides,
and I don't feel like anyone
is eye-to-eye with me;
I have no allies in society,
and I am afraid
of non-existence,
of the consequences
of all the mediocre
decisions
of millions.

BLANK PAGE

It's a blank page;
it hasn't butchered skin between fingers
yet.

BROKEN EMPATH

Unbroken lovers
smile at the quiet between them,
the whole and complete
trust that there is
and will never be
another comfort
like the love of the other...

it's nice to feel
that it exists.

HAPPY PLACE

Tonight I let my hair
smell wild as a campfire,
little sticky, tangling strands
salted by a tipsy drip of wine,
and there was a tune
and a warm sunset.

And then,
a moon
and poems.

SHARED FEATHERS

Don't lure me into a cage
with pretty songs
and bright feathers
that have never felt
the wind in flight;
take a tattered one
from my wild wing,
let's breathe deep
and fly,
oh, come away
with me tonight.

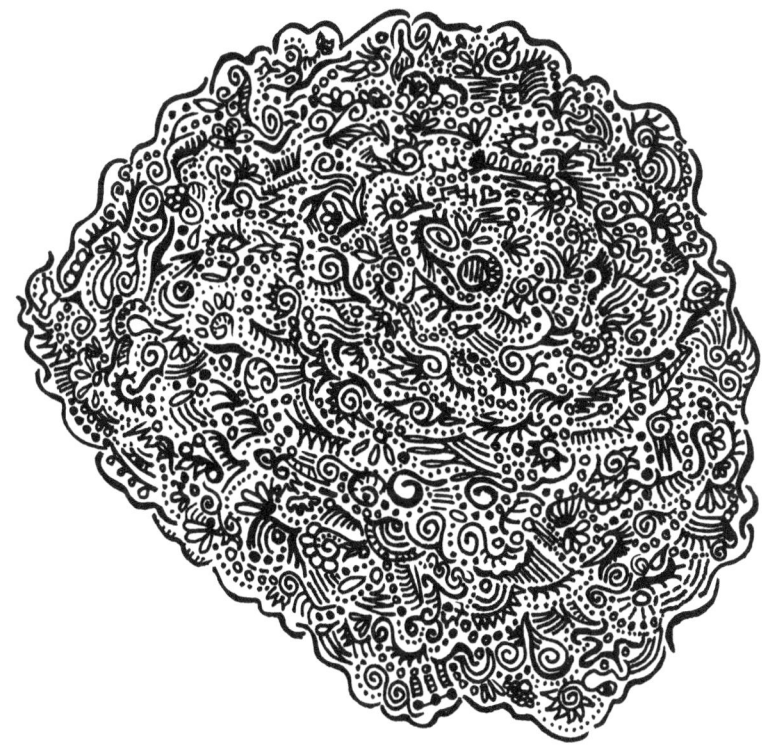

I DON'T HATE THEM

I don't hate her.
I don't hate him.
They are
the whoms I'm from,
and no matter what they did,
or did not give,
or that they'd thrash
and hit,
and then get rid of me,
despite all of it,
I never could hate them,
nope,
not one bit.

I'm hurt,
and I'm mad
that I had to grab
for the crumbs
that they scattered,
a pigeon pecking up
scraps dropped in cracks
by the people I loved,
and I dug for every speck
despite their whims,
deep-down with everything
I was;
even when they could not
or would not
love me back—
through all of that—
I could not have

less love for them.

I'm trying to forgive.
trying to heal within,
figuring out
how to feel the things
they chose not to teach
when I was learning to live;
hug my own kids
and remember that my parents
were the products
of love they didn't get;
little pigeons starved
and feathers stripped.

I don't hate them,
not then,
not now,
not one bit.

But, I have to do better
than they did.

DROP HIM

Don't apologize.

Alight the pile of pictures,
old tickets, carnival prizes,
and wave good-bye.

The end.

I SURVIVE BAD DREAMS

The mushy sludge
floods my toes, I sink
ankle-deep in the sidewalk,
my feet too heavy to lift—
teeth chipped in grit
to get those knees up
high enough to escape
the madmen chasing me;
they hear me heavy-breathing
and dragging my weaknesses
in reflections
that implode the windows,
the scrapes bleeding
and leaving a scent for them
along the darkness.

I hear them screeching,
licking the walls
and crunching the shards
just yards
behind me.

MOOOOVE, knees and hips…
just keep reaching,
don't you quit,
and we're gonna make it
to freedom.

Fuck you, demons.

SPECK

Little speck
afloat on the breaths
feet leave behind
when they rush out of the room

dust scattered
by the hooks and uppercuts
he landed before he fled

kicked back adrift, dancing
a two-step, side-step what-was
around everything that is,
but will never be safe enough

a hand-waving brush
missing the dresser ledge,
the bed pillows and lampshade,
repelled by the curtains
and windowsill,
spun by ghosts
in tornado gusts
around all the restful places.

I really like talking about him,
but so does he, obsessively,
without ever asking about me—
who I am
or what shade I bleed—
so I blow a scream

dodge and duck that he maybe,

might be another one
swindling my empathy.

Is that a love-bomb combo
followed by a back-fist chip
out of my pricetag
so that he can empty me
at a reduced fee,
and then kick me to the curb?

I swing back
and set me free,
oh, little speck
that doesn't ever settle
on anything.

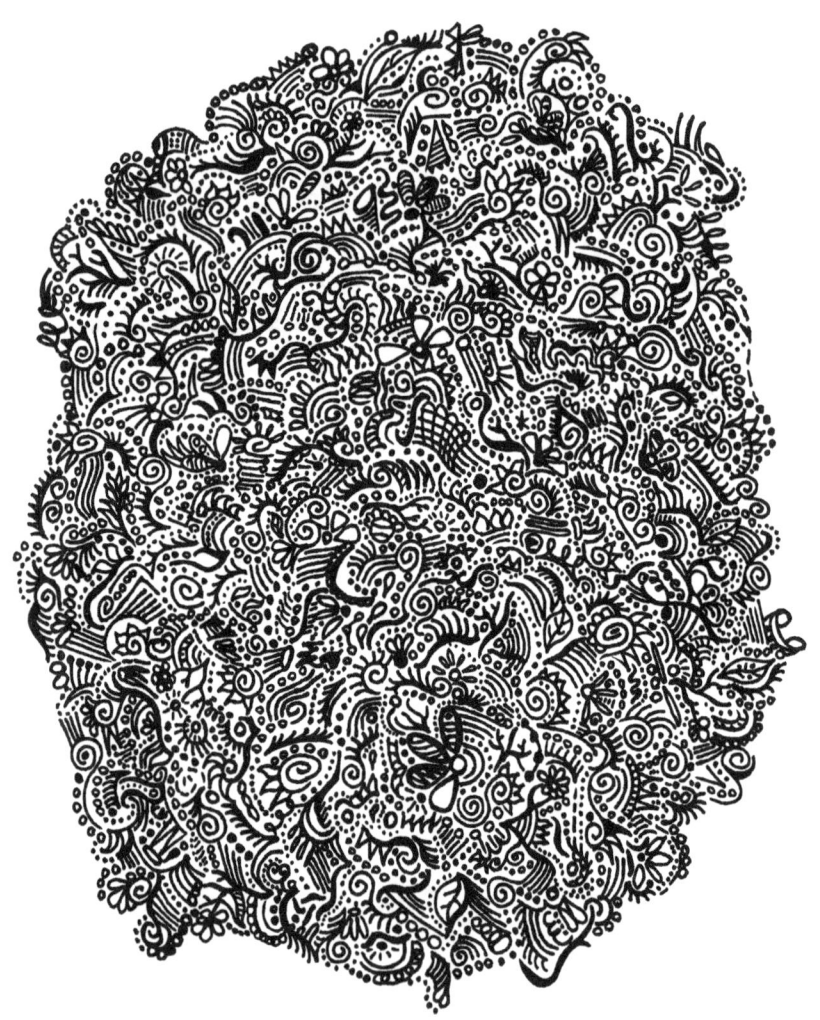

AFTER YOU

I loved you like words on pages;
drowned books with our sweat and tingling.

Complicated everything
with feelings.

Did the best I could
as I jumped in and gave us
more than I saved—
a quarter per sin.

Rolled nickels and pennies
to pay my own way,
carry me through
into who I became:

Not the same as I was
when I left you.

GHOST

I'm sorry if I side-swipe
scratched your paint,
left you surveying
your dented
invented
versions of me.

Outside those visions,
I'm skidding the road
under my feet;
I can't stay awake
because I'm not sleeping,
rumbling at the edge
of my lane, deflated,
carrying the weight
of everything;
depleted, no leftover energy
to coddle or carry
the people I'm dating.

NORMAL MORTAL

Give me gory horror,
make me close my eyes
an extra-long blink;
uncomfortable in my seat
when the portal opens, and
I will immerse in that
virus spreading the undead,
totally fucked,
hiding in a closet
with my own hand
holding my own breath
while the threat,
a creature so abnormal
he will bite or stab
or splay me with a chainsaw,
I become the victim
of his disorder;

his footsteps place my doom
three thumps away
down the hallway of my room—

I melt into that sensation,
I am that dread,
and my pending death,
somehow,
makes me feel
like a normal
mortal.

SHE LOVES ME (MAYBE)

I loved *you*,
it doesn't matter—
it never mattered
which petal
I pulled off
whatever flower
last.

HEART DISEASE

She's a multiple-choice bubble
you barely filled in;
darker than the next one
but not a solid decision.

Just enough ink to mark the page
"maybe"
as you masturbate
to your misperceptions of her
pictures.

Shallow, flaccid beat:
Heart disease.

She is me
and we would rather be
alone.

GRIEVING

It's a privilege
to hurt this much,
to feel
this full-body screaming
numbness;
this puncturing of flesh
and reason
and reality
by blades forged of
empty space and silence;
this retracing our steps,
rewatching the seasons
like we went by in seconds,
replaying the secrets
that, now, only I am left
to save;
so I clean the cuts,
redress, and brace
for the rest,
the next wave of this pain;
it's a privilege
to hurt this way.

OLD PAGES

You can't dog-ear old pages,
The corner cracks apart,
a scrap of heart pinched
between thumb and finger
with no good reason to keep it.

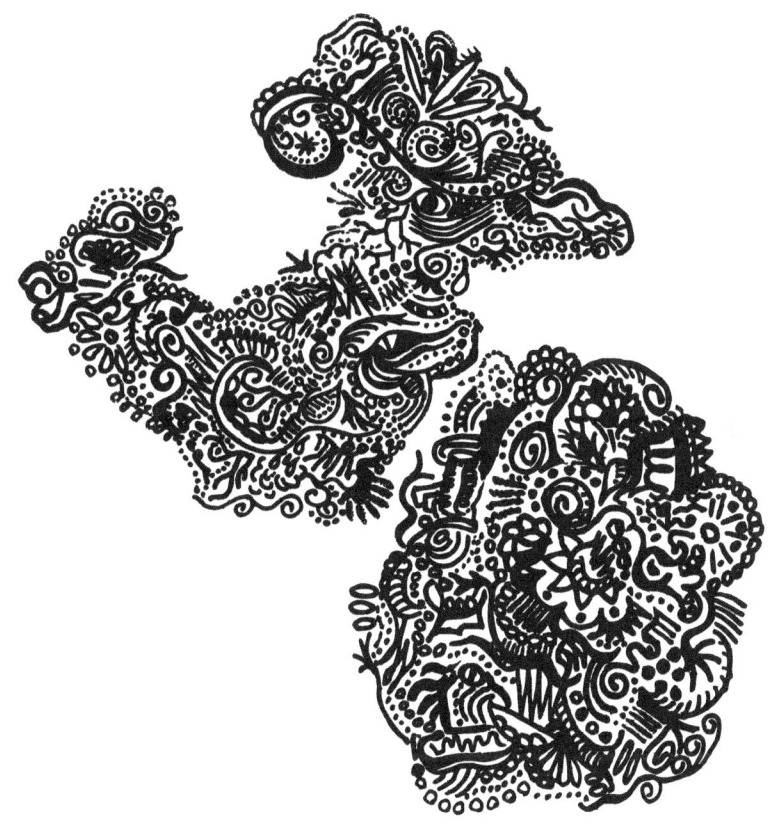

I GO QUIET

I go quiet
when too many syllables
battle for the offering plate—
the raging string
of my sensitivities
to your scent and skin,
your seemingly genuine
hours-long conversations
and how they bend me to crave
us—
and then your sting,
what it breaks,
every single time
I let hope slip,
scream, dream, or smile
about it;
you leave, anyway.

I snuff out the sizzling
chatter,
choose no sounds
to vibrate,
because none of the rests
or stresses,
not mingling
or pounding together
any sentences
whispered or sang
in any dialect
or octave range,
not a single crest or trough

will matter;
no, not even a skin flake of you
will change.

And so,
I go quiet.

IT IS WHAT IT IS

"It is what it is"
means that It
is not at the ends of my reins,
so there's no reason
to waste emotion
on It.

I'm sad as fuck
anyway,
all stuffed up
and raining all over this
might have been.

It is empty space.
It is
fell right on my face.
It is the disappointment
I painted
like a mustache
on family portraits
feigning the stairway.

It is history
we cannot change,
the stories
we are buried in.

It rapes
our Crayola gardens,
It breaks
and makes shards

42

of all the things
we watered
beneath our rainbows.

We had places to go.

It hates me
though.

It is a fate.
It knows.

It is what it is.

And I am all
emotion.

I'm gonna cry
for a minute,
and then
I'll get over It.

TRUCE, HAPPY ME

Things that make Me happy:

sun and trees,
kisses, hugs, and chemistry,
music and poetry,
coaster roads going anywhere;

with everyone,
but love-deep in my someone,
being left alone
to quiet the storms in here;

creating things,
becoming who I want to be,
fail or succeed,
making peace with my years;

I get to live!
takers who know how to give,
accepting what is
through today and what is never.

A POET'S HUSTLING PEN

I wish I could bleed
more of me into these
scribbles that I dribble
onto paper scraps,
squish into the white spaces
of dinner receipts and food flyers
at the red light turning green,
over both sides
of a coffee-stained envelope
still glued shut at its seams,
onto napkins torn
by the re-swiping point
until I scratch out a drop
and write—
about something or other,
if I could just remember
where the rips were heading
before the pen
dry-locked
and forgot
what I might have meant.

CLAWS AT THE OFFICE

Some of our sisters
are the most twisted
villains;

She brings coffee
when she senses a mess,
a hint of drama,
a speck of a stressful item
on the agenda,
pretends to be there
to just listen,
help you question
while you sort out the situation,
and then, when you are spent
and absent,
she hisses about those moments
she calls your weakness
in hopes that it will open
her next promotion a sliver,
or, maybe,
help her finally sprout a penis.

WE ONLY MEET IN MEMORIES

You are a sad chorus
in the happy song of me,
a thousand happy stories
now tears of memories.

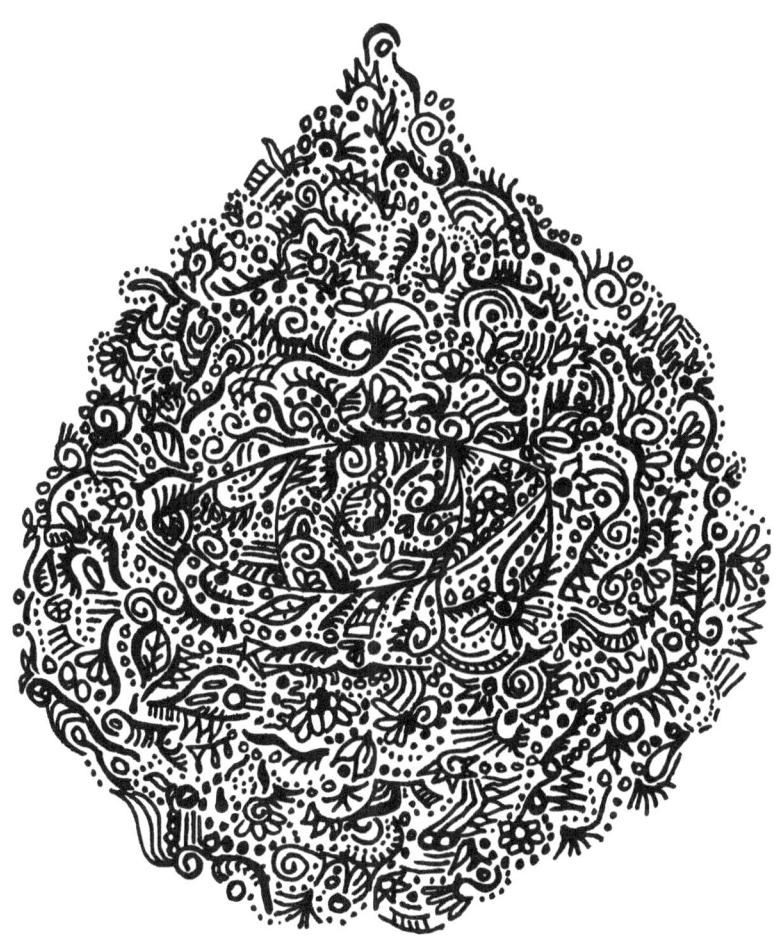

THE LOW

It's three taps
of the snooze button:
stark awake in the dark,
and then asleep again;

then awakening, lingering,
and then choosing the dream
one more time, please;

and awake,
numb in her own
unmoving body heat,
now late
with nothing to dress up in,
no feigning the persona
she promised would mind
the brightening line of sky,
who she vowed would get up
and smile,
just get on with the day.

She tries,
and then closes her eyes.
Not today.

WILDFLOWER

I can smell the softness
of her skin
like drops from the limbs
of daisies, honeysuckle,
and lavender;
cotton dirt,
I make mud with my hands
and build a house with my mouth,
make a song of her wind,
its gusts, in and out.

I bury her perfume
root-deep, and then we
intertwine our stems
and leaves
and fill the wild fields
with our harmony—

I pick her petals:
one by tongue,
the next by poem,
another by the fingertips
drenched in her seams,
the next one, I free
to her moan-song,
and the last—

she loves me.

NO MEDICATION

Sometimes, I die inside
because people I love
are there.

There's no solution,
no medication
to tighten tear ducts
or lighten the aches,
no erasers for the sharp lines
and needle air;
just a chair,
pull it up and sit there
while I flood inside.

Witness this piece of me
that smiles
and cries
and smiles
and dies,
then turns blood to mud
with lullabies and apologies
for almost
being good enough.

The only remedy,
the only way this ever flows
is to let me rip the pages apart,
play those songs on repeat,
let me scream,
let me dance,
let me retreat

to the dark silence
of nothingness
until the rapids slow,
and I float
back
to the surface.

OVERWOKE AMERICA

A pale friend
plugs *her* ears, closes *her* eyes
and yells from hell to sky
that it is sinful and sick
for people with *her* skin
to speak the words of...
replay the notes of...
step-slide in the shoes of
people with darker pigments;
that it is wrong—
treacherous even—
to perform *those* emotions
because of some
lack of experience.

Nonsense.

Unless, that is,
she can't feel the rain,
splinters and whips
that rip *her* skin;
peace at fingertips,
bloody and sprawled
on a battlefield,
scratched into walls
and burned onto pages;
if *she* can't duplicate
those notes in *her* throat,
can't bridge *those* soulful ranges
or make *her* feet step *those*
slide-step, step-slides
to *those* beats;
if *she* doesn't grasp *her* chest

because *those* words
embrace *her* survivor side
and lift it up off the pavement,
if it doesn't make *her*
cry
or fly…

Stop preaching hell to sky
that *we* are different,
that *we* aren't all suffering
this human condition,
wrapped deep, ingrained
in each other's DNA;
yes, *we* really are
the same.

No one needs to be
any further from dream
than to feel the rain,
the rips and splinters,
the ticklish scars
that these parts of *us*
scrawled
and stomped and sang;
what *they* specified
for *our* ears and open eyes,
to breathe it deeper
into *our* hearts
and lives,
and then step-slide,
or cry,
or fly.

GOOD LESSON

Once, we were sun radiating
face skin, and soft wind
melting grass in waves
up hills and over wide spaces,
buttons sliding open,
one and then another,
the urge to root, stay.

Now, we are my B-average
knee scab, the bandaged
skin-slice reminder
I will pick off and leave behind
in some future moment
when I full ripen
and slide off our branch.

STANDING STAGE LEFT

you sweat
the thin web in the dark
where a spark of light
glides and unhides
the sticky thread
only if you shift your spot
to the other side of the path,
if you part with
where you're at

SHARK IN THE SHALLOWS

You splash your foam
over my shiny pebble beach
and make warm toes sink
in the cloudy surf,
twist in the seaweed;
you make grains of homes
and mountains,
melt castles into their moats
as you recede.

I am the specks
of rounded glass
you pull by the ankle
and splash through gasps
trapped and tossed
from barrel to undertow;
drag my bones
a few feet deep,
crack my flesh on the coral,
shake me
between your teeth,
and then
let go…

Set me ragged back
on the blank-canvas sand
of my beach
like you never even
wanted me.

WINTER SUNSET

There are no sun streaks
melting peach to purple,
no daylight gold ribbons
in threads, stitching
the gradient moments
that warm us late.

Today is vague sky
fading gray to darkness,
ice-breath nimbus
hiding starlight, lost
nowhere I know;
there's a road somewhere
under the snow.
And it is cold.

TIE YOUR SHOELACES

You are way more
than the waistline-slash-cup size score
some of these Joes
will try to tag to your toes
and pose you to fill.

Each of those dudes—
ego slaves in the board room,
bar room, and bedroom—
will spill his self-loathing
all over your pretty dress
if he so much as supposes
you might be smarter
or deeper
or happier
than he can impress
anyone to guess he might be.

If you have
more than he has
in anything,
he most definitely will
take your acts-of-service bricks
and mortar of affirmations
as long as you give, give, give,
as big as you will build him;
while he covertly digs,
makes little cracks in your surface,
rips your seams and chips your senses,
erodes you speck-by-speck,
until you are bent and left

alone,
which is exactly when he homes in
because he'll know he's winning,
and he'll start ripping boulders
from your cliff;
then, you'll see it:
your heart and liver shrivel
exposed to the cold,
and then he'll pack those holes
with chunks of him
until the whole dream board,
all the orgasms,
are a big marker scribble
of his last name and his gigs,
things lined up how he wants them,
and on his schedule,
his whims and how tired he is,
and how you don't appreciate
anything he did
for you.

Girl, your purpose
is not a dude.

Lace up those shoes,
crisscross double-knot.

No tags for you.

DEATH PLAYLIST

When you die,
I will line up hours of songs
that rerun our entire timeline
from start to whole lives long;
pour myself three or five glasses
of cheap wine,
and spin through the room
Tasmanian-style
shaking two-fisted screams at you
trapped in pictures on the wall,
curse the holes you will never fill
again;
pour another one or three,
fall to my knees, glass in air:
Cheers!—
wish you were spilled here, too;
oh, I'll chug and refill,
restart the chain of melodies
that pour out our memories,
and sing you until
I either land where you are
or faceplant asleep.

DRUNK ON HIS POETRY

His word-fingers slip my buttons from their slots,
those intentional letters sparkle my spots
and crevices.

My mind sips his thoughts, my heart disintegrates,
melts wetter into the dots of his elongated,
oh, choruses.

BLACK STONE SWALLOWED

I am all that is left of a home
built of moldy, black stones;
the last rusted bone
whose walls are almost gone,
crumbling to the ground
by the heavy sound
of their final silent treatments;
crushed to dust and spores
swirling around the stench
of their last breaths
and then settling on the bed.

No one spoke,
everyone choking
on the same dark chunks:
the stories that are done
and cannot be unsung,
pearls of wickedness
from our mothers and fathers
who were sickened
by the slippery mold
that trickled and eroded
the rotted foundations
of their mothers and fathers
long times ago.

Now they're all ghosts,
and I'm holding my last stone
at the same crossroad:
do I choke and spit spores
onto the poor souls

I bore into my story,
or swallow the onyx cancer whole,
choose to carry the weight alone
in the fist of what I am,
and then take it to my grave
when I go?

Mom, her toes to this line,
coughed and sputtered
the family madness
into our gasping cries;
Dad gagged, wrapped his hands
around his neck
to squeeze the infection
back to the surface;

Both faces purple and strained
as they sprayed their dirt,
their hurt and pain,
as they refused
to suffer alone.

Here and now, I choose
to swallow hard, retch,
swallow again;
hold my nose and mouth
until the jagged shards,
trapped and smothered,
rip me throat-to-heart;

feed all my energy
to the symptoms of my bipolar
and post-traumatic diagnoses;

suffocate this chorus,
make no carbon copies
of the suffering,
imprison every spore
in my coffin
where not a speck
can settle on my babies.

ALWAYS MINE

I never stopped
trapping your name
in the swirl-sides
of cartoon hearts,
singing songs
from the playlists we made
on Sunday mornings,
the skin-tingled chords
and choruses we swore
to each other.

No pictures were burned
in our break and sever,
no rage holes in the walls
or changed locks at the exits;
all of us
remembered.

I cement these ragged lines
of mis-keyed notes
that wore out
in out-of-synch beats
at exactly the wrong time;
keep you folded twice
among my trinkets,
always mine.

LAST WORD

I don't need to make the last sound,
you can speak it, yell it, growl it;
think the final thought about it,
rip your exclamation point
onto the trifold paper
and then drop it in a crowd
to tell the world about us
and all the wrong I did.

my knife doesn't have to cut
the bloodiest deepness of your being
to free me; I don't need you to bleed.
I am done, my love; you won:
the world can believe your story
and you keep the royalties.
All I want—please—is the arbor knot
locking my ankles undone
and, I promise, I'll run.

THE JOURNEY

Our shuffle caves the pavement
right-after-left over 10,005 days
of aching fingers stretched
toward the space ahead,
a finish line we squint to define
with the maroon ink
of parasite memories.

Shoes drag and slide,
left, and then right
blistering the inches
of oh-so tiny increments
through the seconds
and lifetimes.

Each movement matters:
every inch-sliver of road river
we storm into mud
is a won battle.

Mud in the treads is progress,
every taken step
is success.

QUICKSAND

His salt-water syllables
surf the aqua-emerald foam
from the bright slice
between Earth and sky
into misted-rainbow lassos
that disguise the beach
in sparkly sandcastles
with seaweed streamers
that wrap around my ankle
and climb…

…and weave
as they pull me underneath
the sudden rising tides
of his pretty blue lies…

and, as I scream,
he teaches me his disease:
a boot sole
pressed to my forehead
to speed my descent
to waist
to heart corroded
in all its arteries
while he disappears in the mush
overhead.

my eyes, stinging stars,
they fade, go dark,
and then numb,
and, right when I give up
on another breath,
he pulls me back to air

and kisses me there.

For one deep inhale of him…
it's just us:
we win,
and I am saved.

He smiles,
I smile,
and then he lets go
to rub sand in my face.
I sink, blindsided—
How didn't I see
the lassos
in the seaweed?
Why didn't I swim away?

Now, I'm drowning,
fighting for the sliver of light
to reopen...
for space, for oxygen,
for anything but dying…

then, he reaches in
and pulls me up,
but, this time, only thigh high
so he can touch what he wants
while I gulp-gasp for not-sand
to survive.

When he sees me about to stand,
he shakes me off his wicked hand;
under I go, again—
yes, again—
the pit chewing my toes,

suffocating my essence
at the torso
until his grip on my wrist
keeps me out just enough
to beg him—
seeing-stars out of breath,
I beg his laughter to save me.

He pulls at my hand
as his heel gets heavier on my head.
In and out. Saved, dead.
I pray for his saving:
one more folded-palms stretch
out of my grainy death.

He gives me a fingertip
of hope,
a thread of rope
that I now know is end-game,
my last chance to escape.
I grab hold and I don't let go,
I hold and hold and hold
as my sight goes gray
and then black…

but, as he steps back,
he pulls me free to my nose.

I take my breath
and use that strength
to reach his calf—
next breath—
a knee stops at solid beach—
next breath—
and then I grab his thigh,

my temple to his knee—
next breath—
his hip;
I am on my feet—
next breath—
lunge for a fistful of throat
and throw him under me—
next breath—
choke-holding his face
beneath the piss
of his quicksand prison—
next breath—
I do not offer reprieve,
this is not a game
to me—
next breath—
I hold and I hold and I hold
until he gives up
on breathing.

Next breath—
I watch his whole
fucking body
sink.

I breathe.

I stand up
and leave.

THIS IS ALL TEMPORARY

Tomorrow is a purpose
that exists
only if you fight for it
the whole dark through,
refuse to quit;
drag yourself to it
because you have to.

ROOTED IN A CLIFF

The last time I chased a ghost,
I tripped and skinned
my chest to the bone.

Bled my sadness
all over the pavement
as they disintegrated,
like dead;
and I was left to heal alone
in the silence.

I was empty
rooted in blankness,
parched zero
until I lit a little
pure-centered me,
planted that seed
in here
and became full
of peace.

Now, I only climb ledges
for people who crack
their cliffs
to grow me with them;
whose voices echo,
whose hearts are present.

Loneliness feels better
than disappointment.

THE GODDESS

Don't bring hassle to my castle,
and don't even think
of wrinkling your madness
into my pretty princess dress,
knotting its tassels
and ripping its ruffles
with your fragile penis.

You are in the presence
of a goddess,
she is sparkled static magic
and she is not impressed
by your lewd comments;
she does not consent
to your fingertips,
and she will bite your fucking dick off
if you try to strip
even a thread
from her essence.

Exit.

LEECH

Grief is a leech
that never detaches its teeth,
it just sips…from everything.

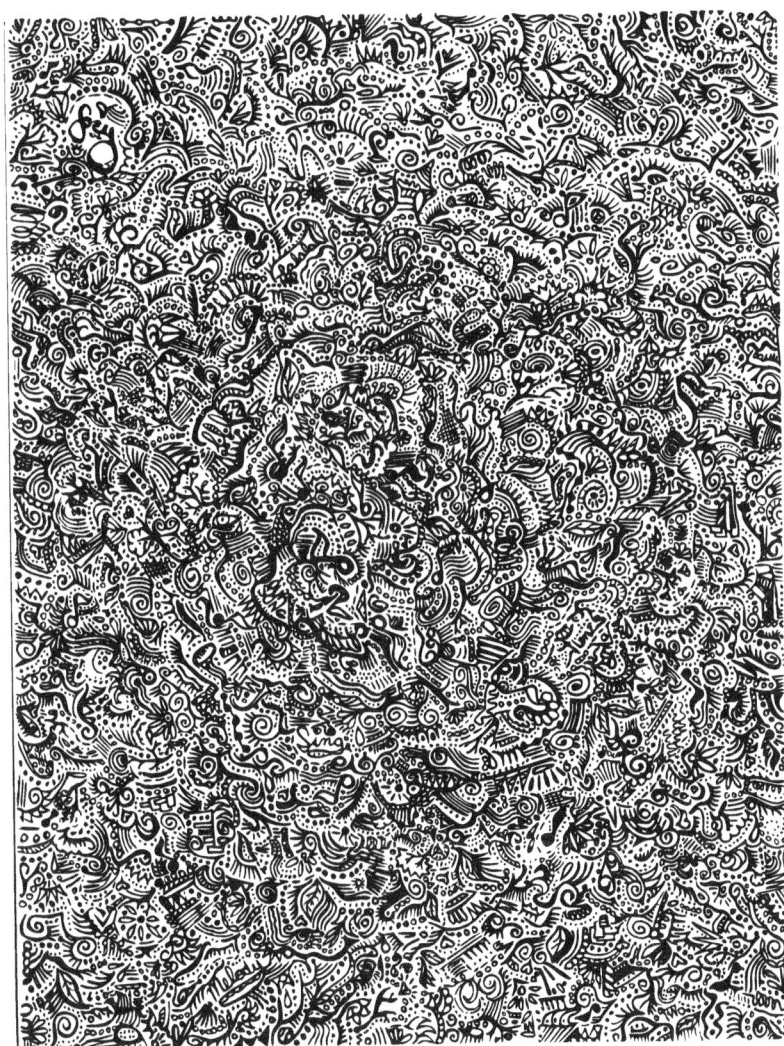

WASTELAND

The earth is already cracked,
emptied through its drain;
a cruddy landscape
of rose and oak carcasses
mangled in ash poses,
last breaths of prayers to saviors
by particles of dust,
unsaved.

POCKET LINT

You knead me into a shield
when your palms flood
and voice crackles,
when you need distraction
or you're not being as good
as you should.

You roll me, crush me,
elongate and flatten
my dust and threads
until you are whole again,
and then,
you pull me from my crevice
and flick me in the trash bin.

OUR STORY

We are the white dust
evidence
of twisted limb placement
pulling all eyes to the stains
and casings,
the charred pavement,
splattered dealings
of little drops of feelings
saved in snapshots
that will never meet justice.

We died in the silence
before the wick fizzle,
became numb to the skin sizzle
way before the shrapnel
severed us into
you…
me…

Now for the piles of bears,
the thoughts and prayers
dingy disintegrating
like the ellipses
ending all love stories.

We…
died here…

END OF SWIPES

All those pictures at the gym
are for him.
Left.

Not a pixel of pupil,
lip, or brow changes
from hugging mom at Christmas,
to playing boat captain,
then thumbs up in the office bathroom.
Is he plastic?
Cut-and-paste head?
Eh—Left.

"Open relationship."
"Separated" or "Almost divorced."
"Roommating for the kid."
Ah-huh. Sure.
Is your partner aware
of this?

Those blank eyes
and that frown-smile
give the impression
that he spikes drinks
and makes stews
out of whoever he meets.
So, nope.

Him, too.
Left.

Oh, a match! I'm in!
And then I go and chat
about my ambitions
like I'm a person,
rather than lay ass-to-sky
in a photo for him.
No good-bye?

Back to swiping.

One pic—nope.

No bio—not a single word.
Nope.

Meme. Left.
Dog. Left.
Motorcycle. No.
Couple. Double-No.
Sunset. Left.

Where's waldo?
Nope.

Settings,
Delete Profile.
Yes, I'm sure.

CENTERED

I love me
like a fresh cup of coffee.

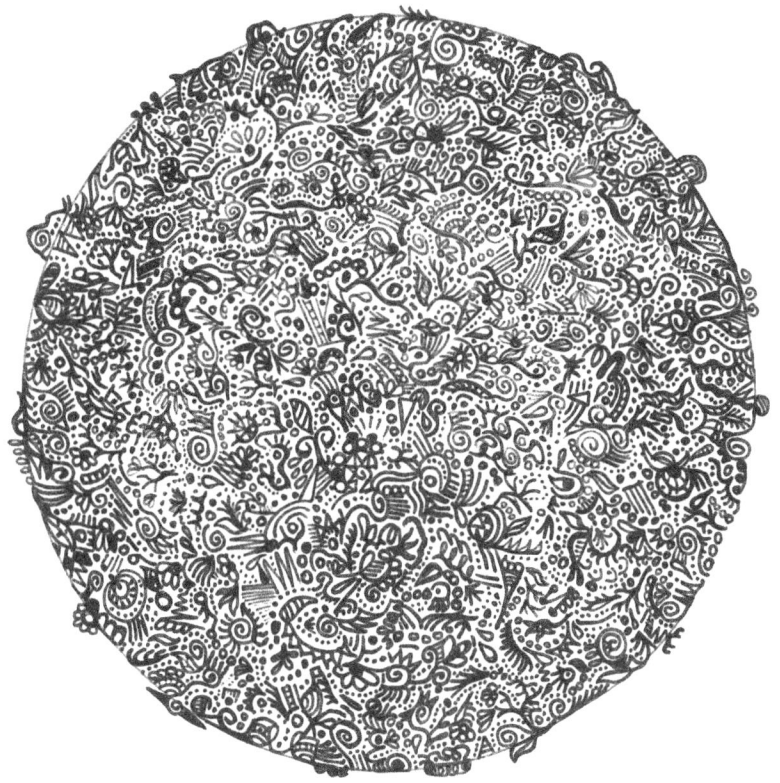

GARBAGE DOGS

Sitting in a cage,
tail between our legs,
we await
the perfect master:
someone to feed us,
who won't beat us;
someone to pat our heads
when we've done
good-dog things.
Someone who sings to us
before we fall asleep,
and who loves us,
even when
we shred the garbage
every time they leave.

ARM'S LENGTH

You stretch your arms,
wriggling your fingers
and twirling in place
to keep space between us,
but, as soon as I chassé
toward open embrace
somewhere else,
you bend at the elbows
to grasp your chest
and feign victim
of our distance.

Well played.
Good-bye, anyway.

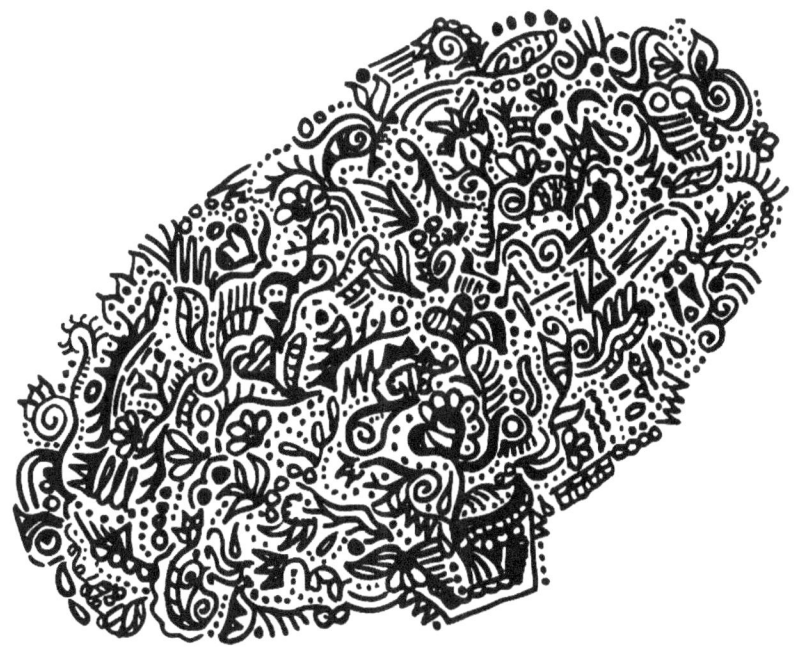

PULL UP THE BLANKET

If 'shrooms and karaoke are music to your essence,
than yes.

If a drive down snake-swerve back roads
with open windows and no real place to go
feels like the right pavement,
than yes.

If your stories and what-ifs turn ordinary moments
into good conversations that convert strangers
into permanent friends,
yes, yes.

If you try to be everything you demand,
both seek and lend
a pom-pom, crutch, and blanket,
yes.

If you can approach love naked,
oh, yes.

If all this…than, yes,
let me fluff your pillow and tuck you into bed.

UNDER THE MUD

I sledgehammered our cinderblocks
to collapse us roof through floor:
burst pipes and glass slivers
mix plaster spores and rock,
mangled locks on unhinged doors,
splintered beds and counters
littered in dust and muck,
covered forevermore
in our mud.

I WRITE POEMS TO GHOSTS

It is dusk, Saturday,
and the wind hushes a bark
from somewhere else;
our stale breath, soiled bed
disintegrating sparks of whims,
the fog wisping in bits
like specks pulled from ghosts
through the open window
that I told you to close.

UTILITY KEYCHAIN

Tough girl.

Wise big sister,
loyal friend.

A sinning mother
teacher
liar
winner
goddess
dreamer
bitch
daughter
abandoner
loner
finger
toe.

Blades of gold
rope,
silvered.

Expressive
frown-smile
with eye liner;
hide and show
as I go.

I know all the codes
and play modes.

Which switch
for your show?

GRIEF, NIGHT #6,935

It is salt in chapped cracks
of empty lips;
no word is word enough.

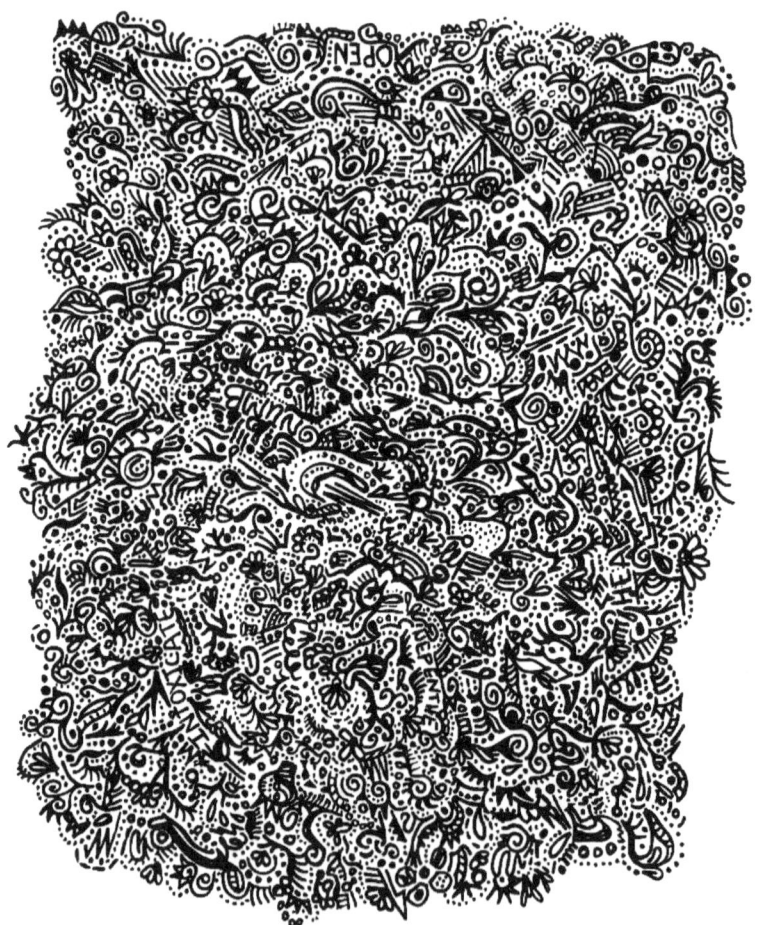

GLASS SLIPPER

Madness, my friend,
is a pebble cracking
my glass slipper,
snagging silk and running
like a tripping twirl
out of the ballroom
and down a hundred stairs
to black mascara smeared
below and dotted above
unveiled eyes,
an unraveled gown,
an un-jeweled crown;
it is hope drowned
in a mushy moat of fear.

NEVER COULD HAVE BEEN

Prisoner of glass;
slow-burnt ink bleed,
a blurry stain
cellophane dream,
an always craved
snapshot in ash,
my never will be.

THE SAME RAIN

We don't belong
on different pages.

Our margins and character spacing
are just shades of painted cardboard:
clouds and trees and spotlights
strobe-deleting every other frame
of our slow-motion plots
scripted on rite stages.

Chant our lines and exit
for costume changes.

We are thumb-smudged
charcoal splices of cotton fibers
blurred at the edges
of evergreen hills and hedges;
watercolor bleeds separating leaves
of palm-tree beaches
from desert tumbleweed,
acrylic cliffs and rivers
stretched across a canvas,
oil-smeared steel tracks
that drown the feigned light
against black and green.

We've been taught
to think we feel
estranged,
so we fist to eye

hard lines between
you and
me.

But we all drink the sun's heat.

Thunder feet to ground,
a stomp, twirl,
tip-toe mis-step trip
through these human
experiences,
spill into this synchronous
masterpiece
mixed-media existence
of us.

The same curtains close;
all paper disintegrates,
every note is swallowed
by the decades.

Our hands embrace,
we bow, catch flowers,
smack a kiss and blow,
bow, wave…
bow…

We crave
the after-storm drip-drops
applauding on pavements
and windows
and umbrellas,
mothers' wings.

We want
feel
dream
chase
need
the same things.

KEEPSAKE (IS BECAME WAS)

It was solid beach
after the shipwreck,
pillow blue skies
dragged behind hurricanes;
warm shards of shells
polished in the sunlight
of each other.

It was happy:
Sharpie marks
on my treasure map,
memories of you there
when you were meant to be,
trinkets blessed to the chest,
buried in the grains
of my stories.

But you were never
going to stay.

We were always
going to break.

Is became was,
keepsake.

THE HEART OF IS

I red-pen every line
of "what might have been…
"If I'd just…
"If…but, maybe…"
and I leave you with
what is.

A FLOWER'S LIFE

A flower in the field
surrounded by grass,
sun over hills
it will never pass.

Rooted, it will be
for all its moments;
beckon bees
with lovely scent.

In the wind, it bends
to dance, to live;
then its life ends
as a lover's gift.

HOMESTRETCH

Here we are,
riding the last trickling grains,
sums of breaths chipped
from cliffs into letters
of stories we tell,
fingernails on glass
we slip and drip faster
through the narrow neck
as ghosts and space
add weight to our heels
we've dug in to brace…

we skid the pavement,
but there's no braking into all the goodbyes ahead.

So let's sit with it,
lift our heads and celebrate
the dead.

Cheers, old friends,
to living this moment
anyway, anyhow;
a toast to us,
right now.

NO ONE HERE BUT US POETS

I hope that if you spark the nerve
to speak your meaningful words
that you are shaking voice to toes
on a stage in front of poets.

IMPLIED SECRETS

Poetry slides an incisor
behind our addiction to living,
rips essence from its bones
and grinds us chunk to paste,
half sustenance,
the rest, waste.

Verses are beds for the senseless
masturbated to perfect sense.

Sentiments and sympathies
in micro-doses
of self-psychoanalytics
affixed to symptoms,
ticks, and epiphanies.

Come inside,
we have odes to sing.

INDEX

WHO SHE IS

Joey sniffs books, magazines, and other paper things (there is brain-tickle in the fibers and ink). Of all the words pressed to her skin, her favorites are: Mom, Poet, and Friend. This former journalist embraced opportunities and bloomed into an IT instructional designer, guiding colleagues to new technologies. Joey self-published her first poetry book, "All Shards & Paste," in 2019.

Visit www.ScorchedFeathers.com for more Joey Poetry, artwork, and technology tutorials for artists.

OTHER BOOKS & PUBLICATIONS

All Shards and Paste, 2019

"It Is What It Is," "No Medication," and "Warrior" appeared in *Blood & Bourbon issue #10*, 2022

"Residual" appeared in *Ohio Bards Anthology*, 2023

"Glass Slipper" appeared in *New Generation Beats 2023 Anthology* by the National Beat Poetry Foundation

"Keepsake (Is Became Was)" appeared in *Common Threads* by the Ohio Poetry Association, 2023

"How She Steps" appeared in the *My Voice Is Victory* anthology, 2023

www.ingramcontent.com/pod-product-compliance
Lightning Source LLC
Chambersburg PA
CBHW070437130626
46553CB00006B/2230